3

D0524689

# INVESTIGATING WITH
# Pattern Blocks

# INVESTIGATING WITH

# Pattern Blocks

**Marcia Miller and Martin Lee**

Cuisenaire Company of America, Inc.
White Plains, New York

MACLEAN LIBRARY
SIERRA NEVADA COLLEGE

To Jared, Greg, Julie, and Bob Diamond—
gems among the polygons

Cover and Book Design: Woodshed Productions
Illustrations: Larry Nolte
Development Editor: Judith Adams

Copyright © 1995 by
Cuisenaire Company of America, Inc.
PO Box 5026, White Plains, New York 10602

All rights reserved
Printed in the United States of America
ISBN 0-938587-78-1
Permission is granted for limited reproduction of pages
from this book for classroom use.

2 3 4 5 -DC- 99 98 97 96

# TABLE OF CONTENTS

## Hexagons

## Symmetry/Similarity

## Area/Perimeter

## Reproducibles

# INTRODUCTION

*Mathematics is one way we make sense of things. It enables us to perceive patterns, to comprehend data, and to reason carefully. Truth and beauty, utility and application frame the study of mathematics like the muses of Greek theater. Together, they define mathematical power, the objective of mathematics education.*

> —*Everybody Counts: A Report to the Nation on the Future of Mathematics Education*
> by the National Research Council, 1989, p. 43

The primary classroom can be a natural laboratory for exploration and discovery. Inviting materials and intriguing problems foster a spirit of inquiry that makes children feel adventurous toward their learning. A supportive, cooperative environment enables children to investigate ideas that form conceptual foundations they can build upon throughout their lives.

Manipulative math materials can be the basis for such child-centered learning. By seeing and manipulating concrete materials, children undertake tasks that would be inaccessible if presented only symbolically. They construct their own mathematical meaning, thus becoming more confident, self-directed learners who are able to find ways to solve problems they never saw before.

Many manipulative math materials are currently available to support this hands-on approach to learning. Some, such as Base Ten Blocks and Geoboards, are most useful for exemplifying specific math concepts. Others have broader applications. Pattern Blocks, perhaps the most aesthetically pleasing material of all, is such a manipulative. This versatile material enables children to examine concepts across many strands of mathematics.

Pattern Blocks are a collection of 6 polygons, each with its own color. A full set contains 25 yellow hexagons, 25 orange squares, 50 green equilateral triangles, 50 red trapezoids, 50 tan rhombuses, and 50 blue rhombuses. The sides of all the blocks are 1 inch long except for the long base of the trapezoid, which is 2 inches long.

Pattern Blocks were developed by the Elementary Science Study (ESS) staff in the early 1960s to explore flat patterns. Today, these blocks are a familiar sight in many classrooms. Children combine the Pattern Blocks to create designs, tall towers, winding roads, and colorful buildings. These activities, and a rich variety of others, give children the opportunity to investigate Pattern Block attributes and spatial relationships, make estimates, and explore number, measurement, and geometry. In so doing, children can make the connections that help them to understand mathematical ideas. As they build a solid foundation of mathematical ideas, children also develop a positive and proactive approach to learning.

©1995 Cuisenaire Co. of America

# ABOUT THIS BOOK

For an overview of **Investigating with Pattern Blocks**, look through the table of contents. You will notice that the book has six clusters of activities.

**Getting to Know You** allows children to explore and interact with Pattern Blocks in a playful way. The intent is to channel children's natural curiosity and creativity so that they recognize key characteristics of the blocks. In **Creative Designs**, children use Pattern Blocks as artistic tools to create original figures. Once the figures are created, children analyze, compare, contrast and, most of all, communicate what they notice. In **Estimation** children use Pattern Blocks to estimate quantities and make predictions. **Hexagons, Symmetry/Similarity**, and **Area/Perimeter** provide children with further opportunities to use Pattern Blocks for learning concepts and skills through games and small-group investigations.

Now open to any activity. Each has a left-hand page of ideas for you, the teacher, and a right-hand page for your students. The teacher page gives a quick summary of what children will do and a list of *Math Links* that relate the key elements of the activity to broad mathematical strands. The rest of the teacher page is divided into three sections: *Start-Up, Wrap-Up,* and *Follow-Up*. The suggestions you will find there are intended to help you and your students get the most from the activity.

The activity pages are meant to be reproduced for each child. Children can sometimes work directly on the page; more often, they will require more space. The ➤ symbol, which appears at the bottom of each page, signals a critical thinking or summarizing question. Invite children to respond to this question in writing, by drawing, or in a group discussion. You may occasionally want to use the question as the basis for a homework assignment.

Activities vary in complexity and are not, for the most part, arranged in order of difficulty. They can be used in learning centers or with a whole class working in pairs or small groups. Activities are designed so that they can be done in one session. Often, however, children will enjoy doing them again and again throughout the year.

The last section of the book contains reproducible pages designed for use with the Pattern Blocks. The triangle grid paper and inch dot paper are of the same size and proportions as the blocks themselves, which enables children to record ideas easily.

©1995 Cuisenaire Co. of America

# TEACHING TIPS

We offer these tips based on our own classroom experiences with children as they investigated with Pattern Blocks. We hope you find them helpful.

- ◆ A major goal inherent in every activity is the encouragement of communication.

- ◆ Allow children time to talk, describe, ask questions, explain, and justify.

- ◆ Take time to share a child's unique questions, solutions, and discoveries with the whole class.

- ◆ Keep in mind that reading levels will surely vary in your class. If necessary, be prepared to go over the activity pages with your students.

- ◆ When we talk about "putting blocks together," we mean putting them side by side so that an entire side aligns completely with an entire side of the adjacent piece(s).

- ◆ We have tried to be consistent about naming Pattern Blocks by color *and* geometric shape; for example, *red trapezoid* or *tan rhombus*. We realize that children may use colors or informal names (that is, *roof* or *diamond*). We suggest that you use both formal and informal language interchangeably so that children can learn the formal terms in a comfortable and natural way.

- ◆ Whenever possible, encourage children to make estimates or predictions and then compare actual results with preliminary guesses.

- ◆ Make an activity into a game by adding rules, time limits, or any other reasonable parameters if your class responds well to this approach.

- ◆ In addition to using the triangle grid paper and inch dot paper blacklines, children can also record solutions by cutting out and pasting the reproducible Pattern Block cutouts on page 70.

- ◆ Send an assortment of Pattern Blocks home in lock-top plastic bags so that children can try investigations with family members.

©1995 Cuisenaire Co. of America

# PATTERN BLOCKS AND ME

**THE TASK**     Children make, describe, and analyze their own Pattern Block designs. This activity gives children the opportunity to become familiar with the characteristics of the blocks.

**MATH LINK**     spatial reasoning; shape relationships; counting

## START-UP

Ask children to brainstorm "pictures" they might create with their Pattern Blocks. List their suggestions. Most likely, the list will include familiar images such as animals, people, and houses.

Tell children to use as many blocks as they wish to make something from the list, or something else that they prefer. When children finish, have them trace their designs or draw pictures of them.

## WRAP-UP

Invite children to look at one another's Pattern Block pictures. Ask:

◆ *What did you notice about the Pattern Blocks as you worked?*

◆ *Did you like working with some blocks more than with others? Why?*

Help children to analyze the class results by posting their pictures according to the number of blocks used in each child's picture. Discuss questions such as these, adapted as necessary to fit the data your class generates:

◆ *Which picture used the most blocks? Which used the fewest blocks?*

◆ *How many pictures used fewer than 10 blocks? How many used between 15 and 20 blocks?*

◆ *About how many blocks do most pictures use? How can you tell?*

◆ *Is there anything about the graph that surprises you? Explain.*

## FOLLOW-UP

Have children brainstorm other ways to sort and classify their Pattern Block pictures. For example, they might sort by kinds of figures (that is, people, animals, toys, buildings) or by types of blocks used most often.

# Pattern Blocks and Me

Make a picture with Pattern Blocks.

Think of something special to show.

Record how many blocks you used.

Then draw and color your picture.

 Show your picture to another child.
Compare pictures.

©1995 Cuisenaire Co. of America

# BUILDING ROADS

THE TASK    Children build roads with Pattern Blocks. They learn that the particular ways that Pattern Blocks fit together can influence pattern and direction.

MATH LINK    spatial reasoning; shape relationships; patterns

## START-UP

Have children visualize and describe the roads in their neighborhoods. Ask: *If you were making a map of your neighborhood, would all the roads be straight? Would any roads curve? Would any cross each other?*

Tell children they will be building roads with Pattern Blocks, and will need to keep a record of their roads so they that can compare and discuss their work. Suggest that children can leave their roads intact, draw pictures, or write about what they have built.

## WRAP-UP

Have children share their work. Encourage children to explain what a straight road means to them. (Some children may say that a straight road must have straight sides; others may not.)

Help children to discuss their structures by asking questions such as:

   ◆ *Which blocks are good for making straight roads? Why?*

   ◆ *Which blocks are good for making roads that get wider? Why?*

   ◆ *Which blocks are good for making roads that change direction? Why?*

   ◆ *Do your roads have patterns? Describe them.*

## FOLLOW-UP

Have children work in pairs or small groups to build roads that intersect, or cross.

# Building Roads

Build roads.

Use only one kind of
    block for each road.

Make your roads turn.

Make your roads wider.

Build roads with more than
    one kind of block.

 Which blocks were best for building roads? Why?

©1995 Cuisenaire Co. of America

# BUILDING WALLS

**THE TASK**    Children continue their informal investigation of Pattern Blocks by constructing walls. This activity helps children to understand how various combinations of Pattern Blocks can go together in different ways.

**MATH LINK**    spatial reasoning; shape relationships; patterns

## START-UP

Discuss walls and why we need them. Ask children to describe different walls they have seen.

Have children leave their walls intact so that other children can compare and discuss them or suggest that children draw pictures or write about their walls.

## WRAP-UP

Invite children to share their work with the class. Have them discuss their structures by asking questions such as:

- *How many different ways did you find to make walls?*
- *Which blocks are good for making walls? Why?*
- *Are there any blocks that don't work well for making walls? Why?*
- *Is making a wall easier, harder, or about the same as making a road? Explain.*
- *Do your walls have patterns? Describe them.*

## FOLLOW-UP

Have children work in small groups or pairs to build a town. When everyone is ready, have groups or pairs describe what they have built.

# Building Walls

Build walls.

Use only one kind of block for each wall.

Make your walls higher.

Build walls with more than one kind of block.

 Which blocks were best for building walls?  Why?

©1995 Cuisenaire Co. of America

# NO PEEKING

*THE TASK*    Children identify Pattern Blocks that they touch but can't see. In the process, children are required to use shape rather than color to discriminate among the different three-dimensional blocks.

*MATH LINK*    spatial reasoning; shape relationships; tactile discrimination; language skills

## START-UP

Each pair of children will need an opaque bag containing a handful of Pattern Blocks. You will need one also. Have children watch as you put your hand in a bag and choose a block. Describe what you feel. For example: *I feel 4 sides, so this can't be a triangle. The corners aren't square. They feel very pointy. The piece feels skinny.*

Ask children what piece they think you might be holding. Take out the block to verify their guess.

For the second part of the activity, name the piece you are looking for. Reach into the bag to search for that piece. Model your process of figuring out how to find it. For example, if you were looking for a square, you might say: *This has 4 sides and 4 corners like a trapezoid. But the corners feel square and its sides feel the same length, so it can't be a trapezoid.*

Call on volunteers to finish the thinking process that you began.

## WRAP-UP

Have children share their strategies for identifying the blocks. Discuss which part of the activity was easiest or hardest, and why. Ask questions such as:

- ◆ *What are all the things you could say about a tan rhombus?*
- ◆ *Which block was the most difficult to identify? The easiest? Why?*

## FOLLOW-UP

Have children play "I'm Thinking of a Pattern Block." One child describes a Pattern Block by its attributes and other children try to deduce which block it is. Children can make up other games by inventing simple rules and ways to keep score.

# No Peeking

Work with a partner.
Take turns.

Reach into a bag *without* looking.
Grab a Pattern Block.
Feel it.
Tell your partner which block it is.
Say how you know.
Then pull it out and check.

Now, think of a Pattern Block first.
Reach into the bag *without* looking.
Find that block.
Tell how you know you have found it.
Then see if you are right.

 What hints could you give to teach this game to
another child?

©1995 Cuisenaire Co. of America

# MORE THAN ONE WAY

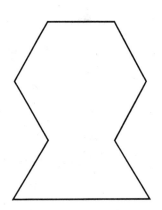

*THE TASK*   Children find multiple solutions for filling a given outline. As children work, they have the opportunity to discover the equivalent relationships among the Pattern Blocks.

*MATH LINK*   spatial reasoning; part-whole/equivalence

## START-UP

Use a hexagon and and a trapezoid to make the following shape and trace it on a transparency.

Display your outline on an overhead projector. Ask a volunteer to fill the outline with Pattern Blocks. Invite another child to fill the outline in a different way. Ask the children how the two solutions are different and how they are alike.

Model how to record the pieces by color; for example, 1 red and 1 yellow, or 9 greens.

## WRAP-UP

As children solve this problem, they will discover some equivalent relationships among Pattern Blocks. For instance, they can recognize that 2 trapezoids or 3 blue rhombuses fill the same space as 1 hexagon. Encourage children to verbalize the relationships they discovered.

Display all the solutions children find. Discuss the similarities and differences among them.

## FOLLOW-UP

Have children work in pairs to make task cards by creating shapes and tracing around them. Place the outlines in a math center, laminating them first if you like, and invite children to work on solutions throughout the year.

# More Than One Way

Fill this shape so that there are no spaces.

Record what you do.

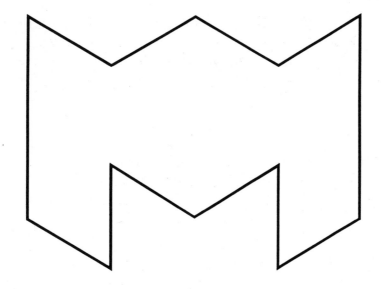

Now fill the shape with *different* blocks.
Record what you do.

Are there other ways to fill the shape?
Find as many ways as you can.

 How could you find *all* the ways to fill the shape?

©1995 Cuisenaire Co. of America

# MY ONE AND ONLY

*THE TASK*   Children fill outlines using Pattern Blocks of just one color. With this restriction, children begin to notice that the angles differ from shape to shape.

*MATH LINK*   spatial reasoning; shape relationships

## START-UP

On a transparency, draw the outline of a rectangle the size of a 1 x 4 array of square Pattern Blocks. Project the transparency on an overhead projector and tell children you want to fill the outline with blocks of the same color. Ask them to guess which blocks will work and why. Test each prediction.

## WRAP-UP

Discuss and have children demonstrate how they filled each outline. Children should discover that they can fill the figures as follows:

Figure 1      5 blue rhombuses or 10 triangles

Figure 2      6 tan rhombuses

Figure 3      12 triangles or 4 trapezoids

Figure 4      6 squares

Talk about the clues children noticed that helped them determine which kind of block to use. Ask:

◆ *How can the outline of a figure help you know which block might fill it?*

## FOLLOW-UP

Have children create outlines that can be completely filled in at least one way with Pattern Blocks of one color.

# My One and Only

Fill these shapes with blocks of one color only.
Decide which color will work.
Write down that color.

1.

2.

3.

4.

 What clues helped you decide which color to use?

INVESTIGATING WITH PATTERN BLOCKS **21**
©1995 Cuisenaire Co. of America

# SET THE SCENE

**THE TASK**  Children make, describe, and analyze a Pattern Block scene. This activity gives children another opportunity to look for connections among Pattern Block shapes.

**MATH LINK**  spatial reasoning; shape relationships; counting; data collection/analysis/graphing

## START-UP

Have children visualize a special place—somewhere they have been, somewhere they wish to visit, or a fantasy setting they can imagine. Invite volunteers to share their ideas about possible scenes and tell how they might create them using Pattern Blocks.

Allow sufficient time for children to create and record their scenes.

## WRAP-UP

Give children an opportunity to examine one another's scenes. Display children's drawings. Before posting, have children count and record on their drawings the number of blocks they used so that the numbers can be seen from a distance.

Start the discussion by asking volunteers to explain why they used the blocks they did. Continue by asking questions such as:

◆ *In what way are the scenes the same? Different?*

◆ *Is there a certain block that many children used in the same way?*

◆ *Why do you think this happened?*

◆ *Do any types of blocks work better together than others?*

Then ask:

◆ *Which scene used the most blocks?*

◆ *Which used the fewest blocks?*

◆ *How many scenes used fewer than 15 blocks?*

◆ *How many used between 15 and 25 blocks? More than 25?*

◆ *About how many blocks did most children use? Why do you think so?*

## FOLLOW-UP

Have each child choose a classmate's scene and try to replicate it with Pattern Blocks.

# Set the Scene

Make a picture with Pattern Blocks.

Think of one special place to show.

Then draw and color your picture.

 What does your picture show?
How many blocks did you use in all?
Which block did you use *most*?

©1995 Cuisenaire Co. of America

# FOLLOW THE RULE

|  |  |
|---|---|
| ***THE TASK*** | Children create figures that meet given parameters. This activity requires children to apply their understanding of the shape attributes of Pattern Blocks. |
| ***MATH LINK*** | spatial reasoning; shape relationships; counting |

## START-UP

Pose a problem such as the following for children to solve:

*Use 3 Pattern Blocks.  Make something that looks like a letter.*

Have children compare letters and verify that they used 3 blocks and made recognizable letters.  Invite some children to describe how they worked. Encourage descriptive language such as *tall*, *wide*, and *wider*.

Before children begin the activity, remind them to verify that each solution meets all the rules.  Point out that it is possible to have more than one solution for the same letter.

## WRAP-UP

Display drawings of children's solutions, grouped by problem.  Compare and discuss solutions.  Ask questions such as:

- ◆ *How did you decide which Pattern Blocks to use?*
- ◆ *How did you know when you had a good solution?*
- ◆ *What kinds of changes did you make if your first solution didn't work?*

## FOLLOW-UP

Have children create rules of their own for classmates to follow.

# Follow the Rule

Solve these problems.
Draw each figure you make.

Take 11 Pattern Blocks.
Make something that comes to a point.

Take 12 Pattern Blocks.
Make something with a flat bottom.

Take 13 Pattern Blocks.
Make something with a hole in the middle.

 Which problem was hardest for you to solve? Why?

©1995 Cuisenaire Co. of America

# COVER-UP

*THE TASK*     Children explore the concept of tiling. This activity helps them learn more about the pieces and how they fit together. It is also an opportunity to explore symmetry.

*MATH LINK*     spatial reasoning; shape relationships

## START-UP

Although children are asked to cover a desktop, they can use any large rectangular surface—for example, a table, gameboard, lunch tray, workmat, or carpet sample. Tell children that when they have finished covering their surface with blocks, they can circulate and notice what other children did.

## WRAP-UP

Bring the class together to discuss what each pair did to cover a surface. Encourage children to describe any patterns created or discoveries made. Ask questions such as:

- *Were you able to cover the whole surface without going past the edges?*
- *Did you have a system for covering your surface? If so, describe it.*
- *Did some blocks work better than others? Why?*
- *What problems did you have? How did you solve them?*
- *How were other children's cover-ups different? How were they the same?*

## FOLLOW-UP

Have all children investigate covering a surface with just two kinds of blocks, such as hexagons and triangles, squares and trapezoids, or blue and tan rhombuses. Children can decide how they will record their results. Compare solutions. Repeat, but have children use two new kinds of blocks this time. Discuss the advantages and disadvantages of using the various combinations for covering a surface.

# Cover-Up

Work with a partner.

Cover your desktop with Pattern Blocks.
Use any blocks you like.
Don't leave spaces between blocks.
Don't go past the edges of the desk.

 Look at your cover-up. What do you notice?

©1995 Cuisenaire Co. of America

# COPYCAT

**THE TASK**    Children make Pattern Block figures and describe them to partners, who try to duplicate the figures. This activity increases children's ability to use descriptive language to communicate mathematical ideas.

**MATH LINK**    spatial reasoning; language skills

## START-UP

If necessary, review ways to describe each Pattern Block, using either formal or informal language *(trapezoid* or *red piece)* depending on children's readiness.

Help partners create a visual barrier between them, such as a book, a folder, or a gameboard standing on end.

Model the activity. Be Cat, and have the class be Copycat. Make a figure with 3 Pattern Blocks that children can't see. Explain that you will describe what you have made so that each child can build it. For example: *Put down a red trapezoid with the long side on top. Then put a tan rhombus on the left side of the trapezoid and another tan rhombus on the right side of the trapezoid, going in the same direction. The space underneath the trapezoid should look as if a square could fit in it.*

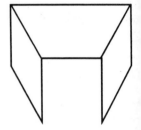

Allow children to ask questions as they try to make your figure. When everyone is ready, show what you made and have children compare figures and talk about the "match."

## WRAP-UP

Discuss what was easy or hard about the game. Have partners share what worked best and how they knew when Copycat had matched Cat's figure. Children can play this game many times throughout the year.

## FOLLOW-UP

Tape-record directions children can follow when working independently.

Allow figures made of more than 5 blocks.

©1995 Cuisenaire Co. of America
CREATIVE DESIGNS

# Copycat

Work with a partner.

Decide who is Cat and who is Copycat.
Make a wall between you.

Cat makes a figure with 4 or 5 blocks.
Cat tells Copycat how to make the figure.
Copycat does not peek.

Partners check Copycat's figure.

Play again.  Switch roles.

 What is the best way for Cat to help Copycat?

**INVESTIGATING WITH PATTERN BLOCKS**
©1995 Cuisenaire Co. of America

# VALUABLE FIGURES

**THE TASK**   Children use Pattern Blocks with assigned values, creating figures worth specified totals. This activity focuses children on the size relationships among Pattern Blocks.

**MATH LINK**   spatial reasoning; computation; proportional reasoning

## START-UP

Post the picture of the 4 blocks and their values that appears on the activity page.

Tell children to make a figure using 3 blocks. They can use any combination of the blocks shown.

Have a volunteer display one such figure on the overhead. Ask children to find out how much the figure is worth using the posted values. Do this a few more times.

Tell children to make a figure worth 6. Invite volunteers to show what they have done.

Have children draw each answer on a separate sheet of paper.

## WRAP-UP

Have children post their results, putting those with the same value together. Encourage children to talk about their solutions. Ask questions such as:

- *How did you go about solving each problem?*
- *Did all the figures with the same value use the same number of blocks? Explain.*
- *What can you say about the values given to the blocks? For example, why is the red rhombus 3 when the green triangle is 1?*

Help children see that the values relate to the relative sizes of the blocks. For example, the blue rhombus is twice the value of the triangle because 2 triangles equal 1 blue rhombus.

## FOLLOW-UP

Have children assign any value they want to the green triangle. Then help them find the values of the other blocks, keeping in mind the proportionality of the blocks. For example, the blue rhombus must be twice the value of the triangle.

©1995 Cuisenaire Co. of America
CREATIVE DESIGNS

# Valuable Figures

Give these blocks the following values.

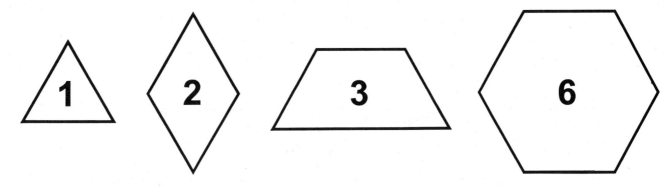

Use the blocks to make figures worth each amount.
Draw each figure.

Make a figure worth 15.

Make a figure worth 18.

Make a figure worth 25.

Make a figure worth between 35 and 40.

Make a figure with 10 blocks. What is it worth?

Make a figure worth *less than* 14.
Use exactly 7 blocks.

 Why do you think the blocks have the values they do?

# TOWER TEST

**THE TASK**  Children estimate how many Pattern Blocks of one kind they can stack, then build towers to see how many they actually stack. In the process, children explore relationships between size, shape, and height.

**MATH LINK**  estimation; counting; data collection/analysis

## START-UP

Ask children for their ideas about the best ways to build Pattern Block towers. Have volunteers demonstrate different ways to stack blocks of one kind. Children might stand pieces on their edges and stack one on top of another, or place pieces flat on the desk and stack them in layers, like coins. Some will probably line up pieces carefully and others will doubtless stack them in different orientations. Discuss with children what successful tower building requires (that is, building on a flat surface, placing blocks squarely on top of one another, and steadying one hand with the other).

Review the meaning of *to estimate.* Explain to children that they will first estimate how many of one shape they can stack and then build a tower to see. Ask what they think they can learn by estimating and stacking the same pieces more than once. Remind children that they should record both estimates and exact numbers.

## WRAP-UP

Collect and record children's results on a tally table. Begin the discussion by inviting children to talk about their estimates and what they noticed about them. Ask questions such as:

♦ *How do the heights of the different towers compare?*

♦ *Did the results turn out as you expected? Explain.*

♦ *What affects the height of a tower?*

Encourage children to make generalizations and comparisons based on the data. You may wish to use the data to introduce the concept of *average* and to discuss the average height of a tower.

## FOLLOW-UP

Have children use more than one kind of block to make a tower.

# Tower Test

Guess how many green triangles you can stack.
Then try it.

Is this more or fewer than you guessed?

Try again.
First guess, then stack.
Write down how many you guessed
    and stacked each time.

Try again and again.
What did you notice about the
    heights of your towers?

Now build towers with other shapes.
First guess, then stack.
Try each shape many times.

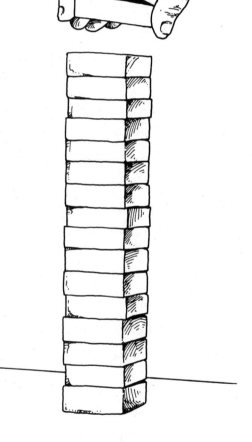

 Does the size of the piece you use change how tall
a tower can be? Explain.

©1995 Cuisenaire Co. of America

# FISTFULS OF SHAPES

**THE TASK**   Children estimate how many Pattern Blocks they can hold in one hand. Children may find that there is an inverse relationship between the size of the block and the amount contained in a fistful.

**MATH LINK**   shape relationships; estimation; counting; data collection/analysis

## START-UP

Discuss ways to approach the task and what a fistful means. It may help to have volunteers demonstrate different methods. For example, ask a child to reach into a container with one hand and grab, holding the hand flat like a tray resting on a flat surface, and using the other hand to scoop, pile, or steady the blocks.

Remind children always to estimate first, then try, and finally record both numbers.

Ask children to predict whether the size or shape will affect the number of blocks they can hold and, if so, which kind of block they will probably hold the most of.

## WRAP-UP

Talk about the results. Ask:

◆ *How did your results compare with your guesses?*

List the number of triangles each child held. Ask questions such as:

◆ *What is the largest number anyone held? The fewest?*

◆ *What might explain why different children had different amounts?*

Discuss the remaining blocks in the same way. Ask:

◆ *What conclusions can you make about a block's size and the numbers you can hold?*

## FOLLOW-UP

Have children repeat the activity using the squares, the tan rhombuses, and the blue rhombuses.

# Fistfuls of Shapes

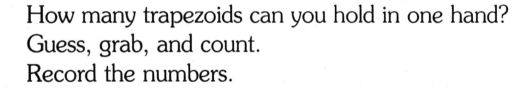

First, sort the Pattern Blocks.
Make separate sets of green triangles, red
    trapezoids, and yellow hexagons.

How many triangles can you hold
    in one hand?
Guess, grab, and count.
Record both your guess and the actual number.

How many trapezoids can you hold in one hand?
Guess, grab, and count.
Record the numbers.

Now try it with hexagons.

 What did you think to help you make your guess?

©1995 Cuisenaire Co. of America

# SCOOP, GUESS, SORT, GRAPH

**THE TASK**     Children estimate, sort, graph, and analyze the results of scooping up random handfuls of Pattern Blocks. In so doing, they have the opportunity to discover the visual advantages of graphing.

**MATH LINK**     shape relationships; estimation; counting; data collection/analysis/graphing

## START-UP

Have children discuss what results they might expect. Ask how children might graph the results, or prepare workmats such as the one shown. In this way, as children physically sort the blocks, horizontal bars appear. Children can then remove each block and color in the matching square.

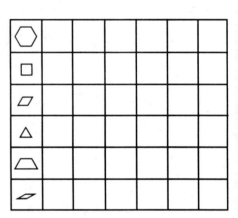

## WRAP-UP

Display the graphs for group discussion. Encourage children to pose and answer questions based on the data. Children might ask questions such as:

- *Which block did you scoop most of? Was this the same for other children?*

- *Was there a kind of block you did not get? Does the graph show this? How?*

- *Which column has 3 more than the blue rhombus column?*

- *Does the graph show the total number of blocks? How?*

## FOLLOW-UP

Have children repeat the activity and compare their new results with their original results. Before they start, ask children to predict whether their results will be the same.

# Scoop, Guess, Sort, Graph

Scoop up some Pattern Blocks with two hands.
Guess how many you have.

Dump the blocks onto your desk and sort them.

Make a graph to show what you did.

 Write about your graph.  What does it show?

©1995 Cuisenaire Co. of America

# AT LAST

**THE TASK**     Children play a strategy game to fill a given hexagon.

**MATH LINK**     spatial reasoning; shape relationships; logical reasoning

okay

not okay

## START-UP

Display a transparency of the hexagon on the overhead.

Discuss the rules of the game. Show the two figures to the right to demonstrate which placement is acceptable and which is not.

Talk about the meaning of the word *strategy*. Invite children to describe how strategy is used in games. Tell them to look for a strategy as they play.

Divide the class into pairs and have children play in foursomes so that pairs can consult as they play.

## WRAP-UP

Talk about the experiences children had playing the game. Ask them to mention anything they noticed. To help focus children's thinking, ask questions such as:

- ◆ *Does it matter who goes first?*
- ◆ *When is it too late to change the way the game will end?*
- ◆ *Can you tell before the last move whether you can win?*
- ◆ *Is there a way to think ahead about winning before it is too late?*
- ◆ *Did you come up with any strategy for winning?*

Some children will discover that a winning strategy is one in which an opponent is left with a space or combination of spaces equivalent to the area of the trapezoid and the triangle. Children should also discover that going first is not a factor in winning.

## FOLLOW-UP

Children can change the game by using several yellow hexagons as the gameboard. There is no limit to the size of the gameboard children can use.

Children can play "At Last" with only triangles, putting down 1, 2, or 3 triangles in any move.

Change the outcome of the game so that the player who places the last piece loses.

©1995 Cuisenaire Co. of America

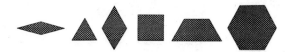

# At Last

This game is for two players or
two teams.

OBJECT:  To fill the hexagon.

START

You need green triangles,
red trapezoids, and
blue rhombuses.

Here is how to play.

1. Decide who goes first.
That player puts a triangle
on *Start*.

2. The next player puts a block next
to the triangle.

3. The next player adds another block.
One side of each block must touch one side
of another block.

4.  Keep taking turns adding blocks.

The player who fills the last space wins.
Play many times.  Try to figure out how to win.

 How can you get better at this game?

©1995 Cuisenaire Co. of America

# HELLO, YELLOW

**THE TASK**     Children find all combinations of Pattern Blocks congruent to the hexagon. This activity gives children an opportunity to discover fractional relationships among the blocks.

**MATH LINK**    spatial reasoning; patterns; part/whole relationships; logical reasoning

## START-UP

Display a trapezoid. Ask children to use other shapes to build a trapezoid that is the same size. Have volunteers describe what they built and record their solutions for everyone to see.

Display the correct solutions.

Establish that these two are not different.

## WRAP-UP

Display children's solutions. They may include some or all of the following:

Discuss solutions and ask questions such as:

- *How many solutions use only blocks of the same color? Two different colors? Three different? More than three?*
- *Are there any blocks that did not work at all? Which ones and why?*
- *How many different ways have been found to fill a hexagon?*
- *Do you think these are all the possible solutions?*

## FOLLOW-UP

Have children name Pattern Blocks by the fractional part each is of the hexagon. They should discover that 1 triangle is 1/6, 1 blue rhombus is 1/3, and 1 trapezoid is 1/2.

Challenge children to give number sentences to name combinations of Pattern Blocks that form the hexagon; for instance, 2 blue rhombuses + 2 triangles = 1/3 + 1/3 + 1/6 + 1/6.

# Hello, Yellow

Fill the hexagons in as many different ways as you can.

Draw and color each way.
If you need more space, use the back.

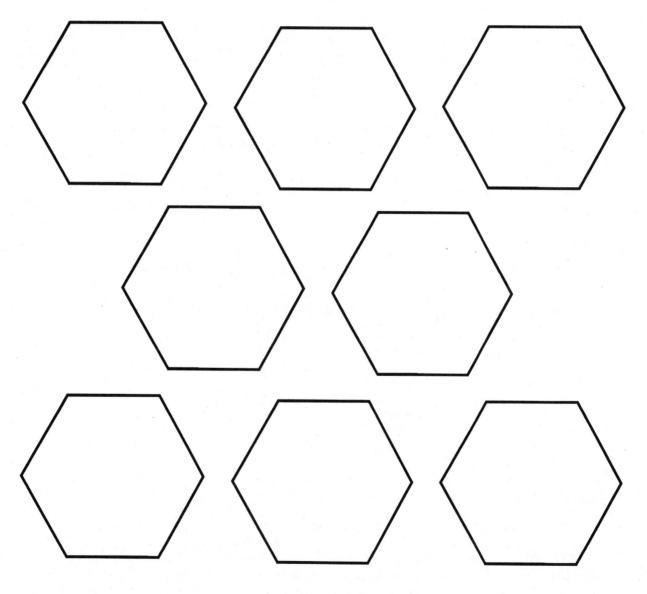

 How can you know if you found every way?

©1995 Cuisenaire Co. of America

# HEXAGON FILL-IN

**THE TASK**   Children play a strategy game to fill a figure made of hexagons.

**MATH LINK**   spatial reasoning; shape relationships; logical reasoning

## START-UP

Prepare spinners like the one to the right for each group.

Display a transparency of the gameboard on an overhead.

Discuss the rules of the game. Tell children that once a piece is placed, it cannot be moved. Players are forced to think carefully about the kinds of spaces left after they add a piece.

Play a demonstration game with a volunteer so that children have an opportunity to discuss strategies and rules *before* they play on their own.

Encourage children to play several times and to look for winning strategies.

## WRAP-UP

Have children share their experiences in playing the game. Ask questions such as:

- *Is this a fair game? Why do you think so?*
- *What is the fewest number of spins it could take to fill the figure? What would these spins be?*
- *Does it matter who goes first?*
- *Does it matter where you place a piece? Why?*
- *Why is the game played only with trapezoids, blue rhombuses, and triangles?*

## FOLLOW-UP

Have children design a different gameboard.

Have children design a different spinner for the game. For example, they might design one that shows different numbers of each block or one that shows more than one Pattern Block in a sector.

©1995 Cuisenaire Co. of America

# Hexagon Fill-In

This game is for two players or two teams.
OBJECT:  To fill the figure.

You need a spinner.  You also need green triangles, red
    trapezoids, and blue rhombuses.

Here is how to play.

1. Decide who goes first.
   That player spins and takes the block the spinner shows.
   The player puts it anywhere to begin filling the figure.

2. The next player spins and puts that block in the figure.
   If a block won't fit, the player spins again.
   If *that* block won't fit, the player loses a turn.

3.  Keep taking turns spinning and adding blocks.

The player who fills the last space wins.

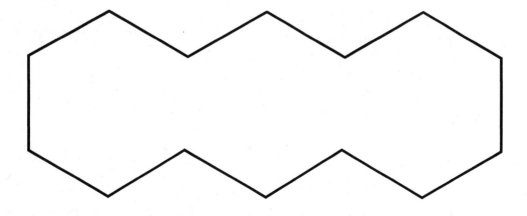

 What changes might make the game better?

©1995 Cuisenaire Co. of America

# HEFTY HEXAGON

*THE TASK*    Children try to find all possible Pattern Block combinations that fill a large hexagon. Because of the size of the hexagon, the importance of using a systematic approach becomes even clearer than in other Pattern Block activities.

*MATH LINK*    spatial reasoning; patterns; counting; data collection/analysis; logical reasoning

## START-UP

On the chalkboard or on chart paper, draw a table similar to the one children will use for this activity but with only two or three rows.

Display a transparency of the yellow hexagon on the overhead. Ask children to find one way to fill the hexagon. Call on volunteers to describe their fill-in and model recording by filling in the table.

Tell children that when they do the fill-in, they will be working with a larger hexagon.

This investigation may require more than one class period. Give children as much time as they need.

## WRAP-UP

Invite children to tell how they went about the task and how they knew when a solution was unique. Discuss how many solutions children found. As children describe a solution, record it. Continue until all solutions have been recorded. Ask:

◆ *Do you think we have found all the possible solutions? Why do you think so?*

To reflect children's different strategies, you might suggest reorganizing the numbers in the table.

For example, the table to the right shows the strategy of systematically replacing every 2 triangles with a blue rhombus. The pattern of the numbers on the table also makes it clear that 2 triangles can be replaced by 1 blue rhombus.

|  | △ | ▱ | ⬠ | ⬡ |
|---|---|---|---|---|
| # 1 | 24 | 0 | 0 | 0 |
| # 2 | 22 | 1 | 0 | 0 |
| # 3 | 20 | 2 | 0 | 0 |
| # 4 | 18 | 3 | 0 | 0 |

## FOLLOW-UP

Ask children to look for patterns in the data.

Have children design other hexagon-based figures that they can investigate in a similar way.

# Hefty Hexagon

Find as many ways as you can to fill the big hexagon.

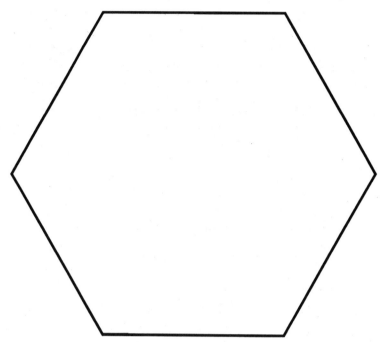

Record the blocks you use each time.
Your chart could look like this.

| | △ | ▱ | ⬭ | ⬡ |
|---|---|---|---|---|
| # 1 | | | | |
| # 2 | | | | |
| # 3 | | | | |
| # 4 | | | | |

 Describe any patterns you notice.

©1995 Cuisenaire Co. of America

# SHAPE COUSINS

**THE TASK**   Children find and explore a variety of hexagons. Through this investigation, children may realize that polygons with the same name do not necessarily have the same shape.

**MATH LINK**   spatial reasoning; shape relationships; logical reasoning; perimeter

## START-UP

Ask children to find the Pattern Block with 6 sides. Tell them that all 6-sided figures are called hexagons.

Display the 2 figures shown on the activity page.

Have children explain why both are hexagons. Discuss the differences between the 2 hexagons.

Display the figures to the right.

Have children identify the hexagon and tell how they know what it is.

## WRAP-UP

Display the various hexagonal figures children have created.
Among them could be the following:

As children discuss the similarities and differences among the figures, make a list of their observations. Ask questions such as:

◆ *Which hexagons have all their sides equal? No sides equal? 1, 2, 3, 4, or 5 sides equal? How do you know?*

◆ *Do all the hexagons have the same perimeter? How can you tell?*

## FOLLOW-UP

Have children explore and build nonregular quadrilaterals.

Challenge children to make a nonregular triangle using Pattern Blocks. Have them explain what happens.

©1995 Cuisenaire Co. of America

# Shape Cousins

Here are two different kinds of hexagons.

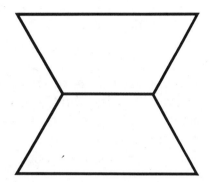 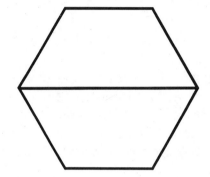

What is different about them?

Use any blocks.
Build as many different hexagons as you can.
Trace each hexagon you make.

 What is the same about your hexagons?
What is different?

**INVESTIGATING WITH PATTERN BLOCKS**
©1995 Cuisenaire Co. of America

# PB SYMMETRY

**THE TASK**    Children explore each Pattern Block for symmetry. This activity allows them to discover that a figure may be symmetric in more than one way.

**MATH LINK**    spatial reasoning; shape relationships; logical reasoning; symmetry

## START-UP

Use identical sheets of plain paper to help children understand the meaning of symmetry as two equal parts. Fold one sheet into two parts of different size and shape. Open the sheet, highlight the fold with a marker, and have children describe what they see. Tack the sheet on the board. Invite a volunteer to fold another sheet of paper so that both parts match exactly.

Introduce the terms *symmetry, line of symmetry,* and *symmetrical.*

Duplicate and distribute the Pattern Block cutouts on page 72.

## WRAP-UP

Have volunteers present their findings, block by block, and demonstrate how to verify their fold lines. Children can then sort blocks by the number of ways in which they can be folded.

## FOLLOW-UP

If possible, provide mirrors and show children how to use them to find a fold line, or line of symmetry. Have children look for examples of symmetry in the classroom.

Have pairs of children create symmetric shapes using 2 or more blocks. Have them trace their shapes and show the line(s) of symmetry.

# PB Symmetry

If you could fold Pattern Blocks in half,
   which would have parts that match exactly?
Where would you fold?

Use cutouts of the blocks to show fold lines.

Some blocks can fold more than one way.
Show all the fold lines you find.

 What can you say about the each Pattern Block
   shape and its fold lines?

# SYMMETRY SAMPLES

**THE TASK** Children construct symmetric figures. The investigation reveals that although symmetric blocks may be combined to form symmetric composite figures, not all arrangements of the same blocks will be symmetric.

**MATH LINK** spatial reasoning; shape relationships; patterns, symmetry

## START-UP

Review the meaning of *symmetry*.

Have children build a symmetric figure such as the one shown.

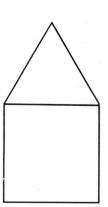

Ask children where they think they could fold the figure and cut it into two equal parts. Use a straw or mirror to show the fold, or line of symmetry.

## WRAP-UP

Have children share and discuss their symmetric figures. Ask questions such as:

◆ *Can you tell if a figure is symmetric without folding it? How?*

◆ *If you add or remove pieces, could your figure still be symmetric? Explain.*

◆ *Are any figures symmetric in more than one way? Show how.*

◆ *What could you say about symmetric figures?*

## FOLLOW-UP

Encourage children to make a large symmetric figure using 20 or more blocks. Children can use mirrors to demonstrate their figure's symmetry.

# Symmetry Samples

Use at least 5 blocks.
Make a shape you could fold into two equal parts.

Draw and color your shape.
Show the fold line.

 How did you make your figure?

©1995 Cuisenaire Co. of America

# WHICH IS WHICH?

**THE TASK**    Children create and distinguish between symmetric and nonsymmetric figures. Using the same set of Pattern Blocks for each pair of figures allows children to notice that symmetry depends on arrangement.

**MATH LINK**    spatial reasoning; shape relationships; patterns; symmetry

## START-UP

On the overhead, use the same 4 blocks to build two simple figures like these. One should be symmetric, the other nonsymmetric.

 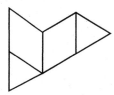

Have children identify the symmetric figure and explain how they are able to do so. Establish that one triangle is in the wrong position. Point out that a *symmetric* shape is one that can be divided into two identical parts.

Encourage children to use mirrors and other tools to check for lines of symmetry.

## WRAP-UP

Have children share and compare pairs of figures. Ask questions such as:

- ◆ *How did you test for symmetry?*
- ◆ *What was easier, building the figures or looking at someone else's figures and telling which was which? Why?*

## FOLLOW-UP

Challenge children to create additional symmetric and nonsymmetric figures that have two lines of symmetry.

# Which Is Which?

Build two figures that are *almost* the same.
Use the same blocks for each.
One figure should be symmetric.
The other should not.

Show the figures to a friend.
Ask, "Which is which?"
Ask, "How do you know?"

 What clues help you know which figure is symmetric?

**INVESTIGATING WITH PATTERN BLOCKS**
©1995 Cuisenaire Co. of America

# MIRROR ME

*THE TASK*    Children cooperatively construct a symmetric figure. This activity helps children to understand the concept of symmetry. It also allows children to realize that symmetry is independent of size.

*MATH LINK*    spatial reasoning; shape relationships; patterns; symmetry

## START-UP

Draw a thick line down the center of a transparency and project it on the overhead. Tell children that they should think of this line as a fold line, or line of symmetry. Place a Pattern Block on one side of the line so that one edge of the block is on the line. Ask a volunteer to put a block on the other side of the line to make a symmetric figure. Take turns adding blocks to the existing ones and matching them to preserve the symmetry of this growing figure. Continue until children understand the process.

Make sure that children sit across from each other as they work to maximize the challenge. Suggest that they can use mirrors and other tools to help them check for symmetry.

## WRAP-UP

Have children share, compare, and discuss the figures they have built. Ask questions such as:

◆ *What did you like more, adding a new block or figuring out where to place the matching block? Why?*

◆ *Does your figure have another line of symmetry? How can you tell?*

## FOLLOW-UP

Change the rule so that children add 2 blocks at a time.

Change the rule so that one child builds a figure with at least 6 blocks touching one side of the fold line. The partner then builds a mirror image of the figure on the other side of the line.

# Mirror Me

Work with a partner.
Build a symmetric figure, one block at a time.

Take turns adding blocks.
Each time you add a block, your partner matches it.

Keep going.
Make your figure BIG.

Work on a fold line
like this, but longer.

Do it again.
This time switch roles.

 Does size affect symmetry? How do you know?

©1995 Cuisenaire Co. of America

# GROW A SHAPE

**THE TASK**    Children use Pattern Blocks to explore similar figures. They see that in similar shapes the sides grow proportionately while the angles stay the same.

**MATH LINK**    spatial reasoning; patterns; counting; similarity

## START-UP

Ask children when they have heard or used the word *similar*. If necessary, give examples such as "Our sneakers look pretty similar" or "Wolves and dogs are similar."

Draw two different-size circles. Explain that the circles are *similar* and ask children what they think *similar* means (same shape, different size).

On the overhead, "grow" the first shape mentioned on the activity page—the square—with the whole class. Display 1 orange square. Build the next size square using 4 orange squares. Make sure that children see that both squares have 4 equal sides. Ask why the squares are similar. Ask how many individual squares would be needed to build the next bigger square (9). Have children verify their predictions by building the square and counting the total number of blocks used.

Tell children that as they do the activity, they should grow each shape, including the square, at least four times and record the number of blocks used each time.

Show children how to check for similarity by using the "sighting" method: Children stand up, hold the original block above their construction, close one eye, and move the block up and down to see if it exactly covers the new figure.

## WRAP-UP

Have children talk about what they did. Ask questions such as:

- *How did you know that your triangles (or rhombuses) were similar?*
- *What did you notice as you built bigger and bigger shapes of different blocks?*
- *Did you have any problems building bigger shapes?*

Invite children to examine the number pattern that emerges as they build similar shapes. For all shapes, the pattern of square numbers becomes evident—1, 4, 9, 16, and so on. Challenge children to use this pattern to help them guess how many blocks it would take to grow the shape once more.

## FOLLOW-UP

Have children "grow" the remaining blocks—tan rhombus, hexagon, and trapezoid. Discuss the problems children encounter.

# Grow a Shape

Start with 1 orange square.
Use more orange squares to grow a bigger square.
How many blocks do you need in all?
Record your results.

Use more blocks to grow even bigger squares.
How many blocks do you need for each bigger square?
Record your results.

Now start with 1 green triangle.
Use more green triangles to grow bigger triangles that
    are the same shape.
Record your results.

Try it again.
This time start with 1 blue rhombus.

 How can you make sure that two sizes of one shape
are similar?

©1995 Cuisenaire Co. of America

# SHAPE STRETCHER

*THE TASK*    Children explore similarity by building bigger versions of given figures. In so doing, children can discover that the concept of similarity applies to composite figures as well as to individual shapes.

*MATH LINK*    spatial reasoning; patterns; counting; similarity

## START-UP

If necessary, review the idea of similar figures.

## WRAP-UP

Have children display their drawings of the given figures and talk about them. Then have children show their own creations. Invite children to talk about the challenges of the activity. Ask questions such as:

◆ *How did you know how to arrange blocks to make the first figure each time?*

◆ *How did you know that your big figure was similar to the first one?*

◆ *How many more blocks did you use in the larger version?*

◆ *What do you have to think about to make another similar figure that is even bigger?*

## FOLLOW-UP

Have each child make a simple composite figure and challenge another child to make a larger version of it.

Have children build a third, larger similar figure for every given figure.

Prepare several large Pattern Block figures. Challenge children to build *smaller* similar figures.

# Shape Stretcher

Build each figure.
Then build a bigger figure that has the same shape.
Draw and color your big figure.

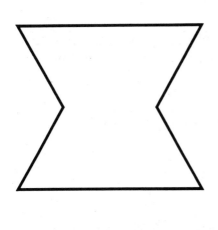

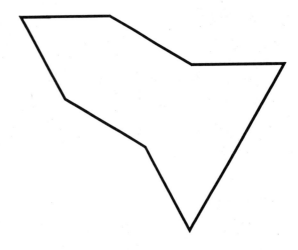

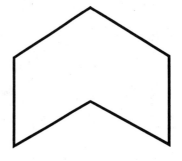

Build your own small figure.
Make a bigger figure with the same shape.
Draw and color your figures.

 How did you decide which blocks to use to make
the bigger figures?

©1995 Cuisenaire Co. of America

# WHICH IS BIGGER?

**THE TASK**      Children compare the areas of irregular figures. This investigation leads children to devise informal strategies for finding area.

**MATH LINK**      spatial reasoning; estimation; counting; logical reasoning; area

## START-UP

Allow children to approach this investigation intuitively. Call their attention to the picture on the activity page. Ask how the houses are the same and how they are different. Have volunteers give their opinions on which house is bigger and why.

Ask children how they might use Pattern Blocks to find out which house is bigger.

## WRAP-UP

Take a survey of how many children think Clark's house is bigger and how many think Hannah's house is bigger. Have children share their reasoning. Encourage them to explain how they chose which blocks to use and how they used these blocks to solve the problem. Ask questions such as:

◆ *Is it hard to compare the two houses? Why?*

◆ *What do you think* big *means to Hannah? To Clark?*

◆ *Does* taller *always mean* bigger*?*

◆ *How did the blocks help you to compare the houses?*

## FOLLOW-UP

Have children make up similar visual problems for classmates to solve.

# Which Is Bigger?

Clark says, "My house is bigger."
Hannah says, "No way! Mine is bigger!"
Which house do you think is bigger? Why?
Use Pattern Blocks to decide.

Hannah's House

Clark's House

➤ Write to Hannah and Clark.
  Tell what you did and what you found out.

---

©1995 Cuisenaire Co. of America

# PB-OMINOES

**THE TASK**   Children find all possible figures that can be made from 3 identical Pattern Blocks. Children are challenged to recognize that the uniqueness of a figure is not affected by changes in its orientation.

**MATH LINK**   spatial reasoning; patterns; congruence; logical reasoning

## START-UP

Display 3 orange squares on the overhead. Ask a volunteer to put them together to form a figure whose touching sides align completely. Trace the outline of the figure. Have another volunteer make and trace a *different* figure with the same squares, following the same rule of sides touching completely. As volunteers try to find other possible figures, test that the figures are different by rotating or turning each one to see whether it matches an outline already traced. Establish that if there is a match, then the shape is *not* different—it just faces a different way.

Explain that PB-Ominoes is a made-up word. PB-Ominoes are figures made by combining Pattern Blocks in different ways according to the rules used with the squares, namely:

*Each figure must use the same 3 blocks.*

*Touching sides must touch completely.*

*Each figure must be different.*

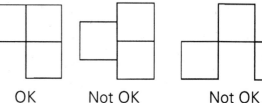

| OK | Not OK | Not OK |

## WRAP-UP

Invite volunteers, one at a time, to post one arrangement for each shape until the class agrees that all solutions are displayed.

Have children discuss what they notice. Start with the blue rhombus, then continue with the tan rhombus and the triangle. Ask questions such as:

- ◆ *How did you know when you made a figure you had already made?*
- ◆ *How can we be sure that each figure is different?*
- ◆ *How can we be sure we have found every possible figure?*

## FOLLOW-UP

Find all the PB-Ominoes for 3 trapezoids.

Find all the PB-Ominoes for 4 blue or tan rhombuses or 4 triangles.

# PB-Ominoes

Use 3 blue rhombuses.
Put them together so the edges touch.
Make all the different PB-Ominoes you can.

Record your work.

Now use 3 tan rhombuses to make all the
    different PB-Ominoes you can.
Again, record your work.

This time make PB-Ominoes with 3 green triangles.

 How do you know that no two figures are the same?

©1995 Cuisenaire Co. of America

# ALL AROUND

**THE TASK**   Children explore perimeter and perimeter patterns. They discover that the perimeter of a row of shapes is not a multiple of the perimeter of an individual shape.

**MATH LINK**   spatial reasoning; patterns; estimation; counting; perimeter

## START-UP

Tell children that one way to describe a shape is by the distance around it. Explain that they can measure length with the orange square. Call the length of a side 1 unit. Show children how to measure the distance around the triangle using the square.

Have children work together to measure distance around each of the remaining Pattern Blocks. Introduce the term *perimeter* as the distance around. Ask:

> *Which Pattern Block has the greatest perimeter, or distance around? Which block has the least perimeter? Which blocks have the same perimeter?*

Have children predict how far it is around 2 orange squares placed side by side. Put 2 squares together and have a volunteer use another square to measure around them.

Ask children to discuss what they noticed.

Make sure children know how to measure around 3 and 4 squares lined up.

## WRAP-UP

Have children tell in their own words what *perimeter* means. Then invite them to share their results and describe any number patterns they found as they investigated the perimeter of the growing "roads" of shapes. You might want to see if any children can summarize by explaining that each time the sides of 2 pieces are aligned and completely touching, 2 (rather than 4) is added to the perimeter.

## FOLLOW-UP

Let children do the same investigation with each of the other Pattern Blocks.

Ask children to predict the perimeter of a "road" that has 8 or more blocks.

# All Around

Each side of the orange square = 1 unit.
How far around is each of these figures?

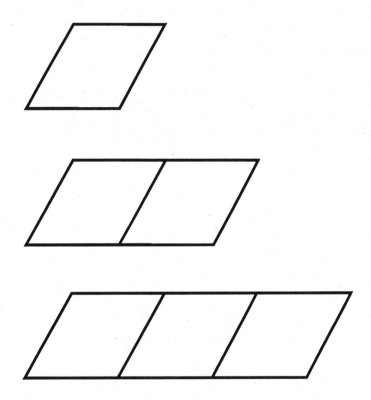

Predict the distance around 5 blue rhombuses in a row.
Measure to see if you are right.

Predict the distance around 10 blue rhombuses in a row.
Again, check by measuring.

 What happens to the distance around each time
you add a block?

# PB PERIMETERS

*THE TASK*   Children explore perimeters of composite figures. By manipulating blocks, children can informally discover that figures with the same area (the same blocks) can have different perimeters.

*MATH LINK*   spatial reasoning; patterns; counting; logical reasoning; perimeter

## START-UP

If necessary, review the meaning of *perimeter* and how to use the square as a unit of measure to find the perimeter of any Pattern Block. Demonstrate finding the perimeter of the trapezoid, pointing out that the long side measures 2 units.

## WRAP-UP

Display and discuss the various solutions children found. Ask questions such as:

- *What is the smallest perimeter you found?*
- *What is the largest?*
- *Can you find every number in between?*
- *Why might someone think all figures made of the same blocks have the same perimeter?*
- *Why do some figures made with the same blocks have different perimeters?*

## FOLLOW-UP

Have partners do the activity again with a new set of 4 Pattern Blocks. Either some of the blocks can be the same, or the blocks can be all different. If you like, have children explore both possibilities.

# PB Perimeters

Use 3 red trapezoids and 1 blue rhombus.
Make as many different figures as you can.
Find the perimeter of each.

Record your results.

 What happens to the perimeter when you make different figures with the same blocks?

# BORDER BUDDIES

**THE TASK**   Children estimate and find perimeters of composite figures. This activity enables them to observe that the same Pattern Blocks can produce figures with different perimeters. Children can also notice that a longer, thinner figure has a greater perimeter than one that is more square and compact.

**MATH LINK**   spatial reasoning; patterns; estimation; counting; logical reasoning; perimeter

## START-UP

Make a figure that uses 3 to 4 Pattern Blocks. Have children estimate its perimeter.

Ask a volunteer to use the square as a unit of measure to find the figure's perimeter. Now make a larger figure with 6 to 7 blocks. Again, ask children to estimate the perimeter before measuring it exactly.

Have children work in pairs for a few minutes. Ask each pair to make a figure and have both partners guess its perimeter before measuring it.

## WRAP-UP

Invite children to describe strategies they used to estimate. Ask questions such as:

◆ *Did your estimates get closer to the actual measurement each time? Why?*

◆ *Were some shapes harder to estimate than others? Why?*

## FOLLOW-UP

Ask children to investigate perimeters for the PB-Ominoes they are asked to make on page 63.

# Border Buddies

Use 10 blocks.  Make a figure.
Use another set of the same blocks.
Make a different figure.
Estimate which has the greater perimeter.

Now measure to check your estimate.

Use 12 blocks.
Make another pair of figures.
Estimate which perimeter is greater.

Now measure.

Do it again.  This time use more than 15 blocks.

 How did you estimate the perimeters?
Did you notice any patterns?

©1995 Cuisenaire Co. of America

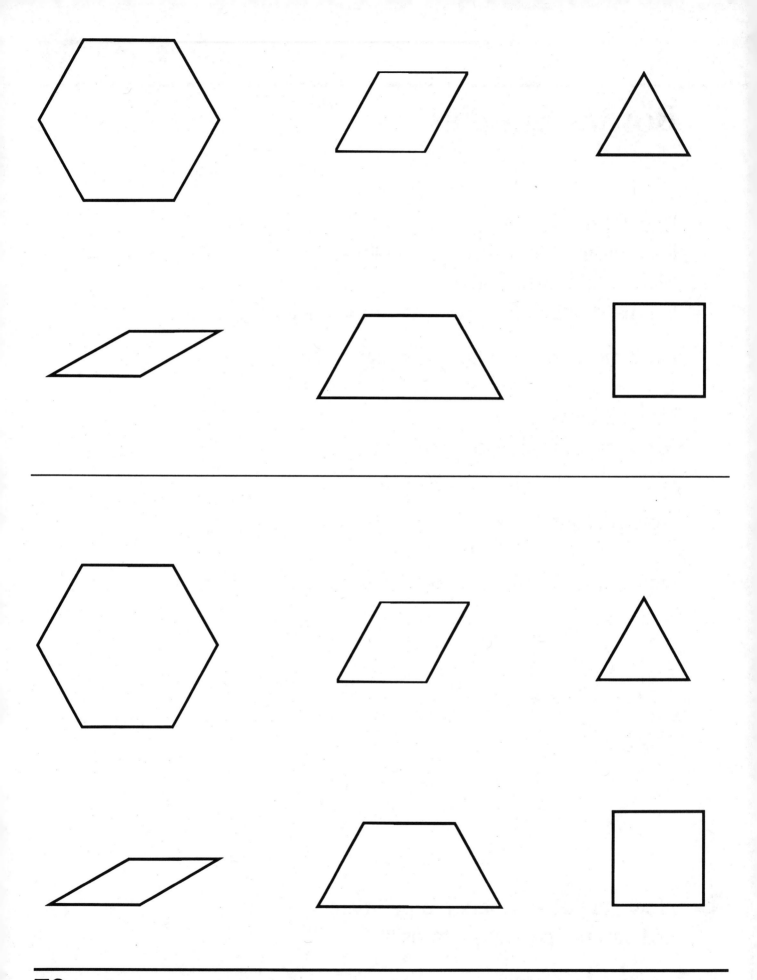

**INVESTIGATING WITH PATTERN BLOCKS**
©1995 Cuisenaire Co. of America

PATTERN BLOCK CUT-OUTS

TRIANGLE GRID PAPER

©1995 Cuisenaire Co. of America

**INVESTIGATING WITH PATTERN BLOCKS**
©1995 Cuisenaire Co. of America

INCH DOT PAPER